GHOSTLY

New York City's Haunted History

GOTHAM

ISBN 0-9700718-4-1

B+T 9.95 11/02

All photos taken by the author.

Book cover design by Jo Butz, *Graphic Design Studio.*

Printed on recycled paper by Sheridan Books.

CONTENTS

☙ GHOSTLY GOTHAM ☙

❀ GHOSTLY GOTHAM ❀

The Customs House site is strongly linked to the history of New York City's settlement.

FOREWORD

Gotham – a fabled city.   Enchanting, magical, legendary – adjectives describing the most celebrated city in the world. Now, add one more - *haunted*.

The Big Apple doesn't seem to fit the category of a haunted place with its bright lights and endless bustle, but New York City is full of ghosts! Her almost four-hundred-year history has fostered an awesome phantom heritage.

From her days as a peaceful wilderness to her prominence as an international metropolis, millions of people have walked her storied streets.

Many city structures date back to the early 19th, 18th, and even 17th centuries. When the physical body passes, where does the energy go? Some contend that the energy imbeds itself in the departed's domicile. When physical changes to the structure occur during renovations, the disrupted energy emerges. This theory could explain some of the inexplicable events that transpire in Gotham.

Others suggest that the spirits of the deceased linger on earth due to unresolved issues - lost love, untimely deaths, or unfinished business.

Some buildings have a haunted history just because of the large number of people who expired within their walls like the Dakota or Twain House.

In the city that never sleeps, neither do some members of her deceased populace.

Peter Stuyvesant still doesn't want to relinquish control or give up the ghost. His peg-legged apparition with its distinctive gait patrols the Bowery.

There are souls who seek to settle the score. Among them, and the most inexhaustible specter is Aaron Burr. His strong political and emotional ties bond his spirit to several city sites.

Many stay on looking for love like the spirits of Gertrude Tredwell at the Old Merchant's House and Eliza Jumel at her Harlem mansion.

Hell's Kitchen cooks up spooks from the past to whet the curious' appetite. The Village teems with shades from her heyday reliving the high life. The ethers of the Theater District thrive with dramatic postmortem appearances.

The spirits of those who have gone before are tangled in Manhattan's roots and help make the greatest city in the world the most haunted one as well. The city's rich afterlife - her spectral wealth of actors and artists, patriots, politicians, poets, and just plain folks, evoke a spooky legacy.

BEDLOE'S ISLAND

There's more than meets the eye at Liberty Island. In 1956 Bedloe's Island, named for its one-time owner Isaac Bedloe, was re-christened Liberty Island in honor of the statue, which stands on the foundation of Fort Hood.

The haunting of Bedloe's Island involves the infamous Captain William Kidd, a respectable privateer living in Manhattan around 1695. He was regarded as a generous, affable resident, and provided the block and tackle required to hoist the stones in the building of Trinity Church.

He was commissioned to captain the *Adventure Galley* and set out with a hold full of New York mateys to hunt pirates in the Indian Ocean. Somehow along the way he lost sight of his mission and turned pirate preying on the copious trade.

He became a wanted man and upon his return to the States in 1701, he was immediately apprehended and executed.

For decades after his death, rumors swirled that the notorious Captain had buried treasure estimated at 1 ½ million pounds on the uninhabited Bedloe's

Island. (Actually the bounty was more likely stashed on the twin forks of Long Island).

Hearsay persisted into the 19th century when the Fort Hood stronghold was established on the island to safeguard the active harbor.

Two ambitious soldiers stationed at the fort decided they would secretly attempt to unearth the treasure. Under the cloak of darkness and armed with a divining rod, the skull duggery began....

Excavation was easy, the sandy soil gave up the prize quickly but not without complications.

As the excited men hit pay dirt, a rush of energy rose from the earthen pit and knocked them to their feet. Then a horrifying, repulsive vision materialized. The grotesque decomposed ghoul, planted a century earlier over the strongbox, to safeguard the loot and defend against theft, nearly scared them to death.

The dead buccaneer remained loyal to his captain and was faithful in his duty to eternally watch over the ill-gotten gains.

U.S. CUSTOMS HOUSE
1 Bowling Green

Shortly after Captain Kidd's execution, the British governor of Manhattan Island, Lord Leisler was also put to death. Viscount Cornbury, known also as Edward Hyde, succeeded him. During Cornbury's term from 1702-1708 he incurred huge debts that ultimately landed him in debtors prison.

The phantom perceived by the grand Old Customs House is thought to be the eccentric Viscount whose place in history is marked more for his style of dress than for his governance. He favored women's clothing and as such his apparition still appears in drag around the venerable building and nearby Battery Park.

The former Customs House now lodges the Smithsonian Institution's National Museum of the American Indian. Some of the museum's one million Indian artifacts include a number of haunted items. The sacred buffalo horn, for instance, allows one to experience the creature's consciousness.

At Bowling Green, Aaron Burr's wraith looks out over the water watching and waiting for his beloved daughter, Theodosia, who was lost at sea.

*Alexander Hamilton's obelisk-topped tomb
in Trinity Church graveyard.*

TRINITY CHURCH GRAVEYARD
Wall Street and Broadway

Trinity's brownstone steeple rises into the sky like a beacon. For decades the famous church was the tallest building in the city. Today, towering skyscrapers dwarf it.

No one, especially not a ghost hunter, should pass by the Trinity Church graveyard without giving the sacred ground a second look. The plots read like a *Who's Who* of New Yorkers who contributed to the growth of the fledgling city. If you get the willies as you stroll among the dead, you are not alone. Really! Many claim more than one supernatural presence pervades the atmosphere.

Eternal rest does not come easy to Alexander Hamilton who has a stylish gravesite here. His young and productive life came to a tragic end when he was shot in the famous duel with Aaron Burr. Those who have discerned his phantom perambulations say his specter seems lost. Possibly Hamilton is confused with his ethereal state.

On more than one occasion disembodied tittering has been heard emanating from Adam Allyn's grave, marked simply - *Comedian.*

*Famous Civil War photographer, Matthew Brady, still strolls
the sidewalks of his old neighborhood near St. Paul's Chapel.*

ST. PAUL'S CHAPEL
Broadway and Fulton Street

Upon his first arrival in Manhattan, Abraham Lincoln traded his beaver hat for a dapper stovepipe style. Next, he went to Matthew Brady's photographic studio. Brady's photo of Lincoln was the first look the country had of their future president; Brady's image was used to illustrate newspaper reports of the budding politician.

Matthew Brady is better known for the Civil War images he captured and immortalized. Legend has it that his specter strolls the sidewalks of his mortal abode near St. Paul's. Sightings of his apparition carrying his distinctive walking stick are common.

Dedicated in 1766, St. Paul's is Manhattan's oldest extant church. George Washington had an assigned pew and prayed here on his inauguration day in 1789 when the city was the nation's capital.

Another legend associated with the chapel is that of thespian George Fredrick Cooke who bequeathed his head to science to pay his medical bills. His headless corpse was interred at St. Paul's.

The poor soul remains behind roaming the churchyard in search of his missing head.

The haunted graveyard at Trinity Church.

Supposedly, the 1831 Church of St. Luke's-in-the-Fields' parish house is a haven for the spirit of one of its vestrymen, Clement C. Moore, author of "A Visit with St. Nick."

Over 200 years ago a woman's body was found in the well that still exists in the basement of the Manhattan Bistro.

MANHATTAN BISTRO
Spring Street

In 1799, while two boys were playing in the marshes in the area that is now Spring Street, they came upon the lifeless body of a young woman at the bottom of a well. The area where Gulielma Sands was found is today's Soho (south of Houston Street).

Amazingly the well where she was drowned still exists. The building that houses the Manhattan Bistro was built over the well, which can be found in the basement of the charming French restaurant

The visage of the long-ago victim also remains intact at the spot where she breathed her last breath. Diners have sighted a female apparition with long hair and a dirty dress drifting about the bistro.

Another odd connection to this story is that the attorneys hired to represent Gulielma's accused murderer, her fiancée Levi Weeks, were Aaron Burr and Alexander Hamilton. This was the only time the two archrivals collaborated. They were successful in acquitting Weeks.

Perhaps this is why Gulielma cannot rest.

More than one specter lurks within this 1880s Mercer Street structure.

60 MERCER STREET

Another stay-behind in Soho is the ghost of famed folksinger and political activist Phil Ochs.

When the country was seriously divided over the Vietnam War in the 1960s, Ochs' music helped to excite political idealism. His suicide in 1976 marked the end of an era.

The turning point for the activist was the violence he experienced at the hands of the overly aggressive and repressive Chicago police at the 1968 Democratic convention. This episode triggered a downward spiral for the singer and after a difficult battle with writer's block and manic depression he took his own life.

Before his suicide, the musician operated a West Indian restaurant called "Breezin" at the 60 Mercer Street location. There are those who swear they encountered Phil's phantom in the place afterward. Plain as day his spirit appeared on the balcony, stairway, and in an office on the lower floors of the corner building.

Psychics attest that another cloudy white specter, that predates Ochs' death, lurks within the 1880s structure.

The ancient English "hangin' elm" in Washington Square Park used for executions until 1819 – the site of many grisly deaths and ghostly legends.

WASHINGTON SQUARE PARK

Washington Square Park is the heart of Greenwich Village life and a favored haunt of the living *and* the dead. Tourists, students and residents join together in the Square to create an international bohemia in a backyard setting. Are the visitors and Villagers aware that beneath the park's expanse lay the remains of 15,000 corpses?

In 1797 the area was a pauper's graveyard and Native American burial ground. Thirty years later the square was designated a military parade ground; cannon wheels often got stuck in the depressions of collapsing graves.

The park was a popular dueling site and used for public executions. Convicted individuals swung from the English "hangin' elm" that still stands in the northwest corner of the park. One of the oldest trees in New York City, its ancient "hanging arm" was lopped off in 1992.

The ghastly history of the ten-acre park is grounds for ghostly legends. On moonlit nights, when all is still, there are those who swear the dead come to life in the venerable venue.

The spirit at Fire Patrol Station House No. 2 remains inextinguishable.

FIRE PATROL STATION HOUSE NO. 2
84 West 3rd Street

Across the street from the former Poe House is another ghostly hot spot, a Victorian-era fire patrol station that is home to Patrolman Schwartz's ghost.

According to psychics, and the account in *New York City Ghost Stories*, it seems that sometime in the 1930s Schwartz took his life by hanging himself on the fourth floor of the firehouse. Apparently he was depressed over his wife's infidelity.

For generations, sightings of a mustachioed fireman donning a vintage helmet and a red wool double-breasted shirt have been reported at the 1906 station. Not only has he been spotted on the fourth floor where he breathed his last breath, he is seen and heard walking up and down the spiral staircase.

One night Schwartz shook a firefighter awake and then stood over the man's bunk and stared. A ghostly Schwartz was also glimpsed in the coal bin.

When the alarm is sounded and the brave men of Fire Station No. 2 rush to answer the call, some of them feel a reassuring tap from an unseen hand, a reminder from an invisible comrade whose spirit cannot be extinguished.

EDGAR ALLAN POE HOUSE
85 West 3rd Street

Edgar Allan Poe lived in many different apartments throughout Manhattan but the landmark building that bore his name stood at 85 West 3rd Street in Greenwich Village before it was razed in 2001. The famous horror author lived in a third floor apartment there from 1844 to 1845 and wrote most of his famous poem *The Raven* while in residence.

But it was not the author's presence that haunted the brick townhouse. A subsequent female tenant, who suffered from mental illness, was kept concealed in the house. (A 19th century approach toward "insanity"). Many believed it was her spirit that continued to live on in the garret.

Inexplicable pounding was heard throughout the dwelling and the sound of a woman's senseless blathering emanated from the attic.

Although the Poe House was torn down to make way for a New York University construction, the school intends to put up a replica façade of the historic house as part of the exterior design. What can't be replaced is the *spirit* of the place – in more ways than one.

110 WEST 3ᴿᴰ STREET

This New York University dormitory was erected on property once owned by Aaron Burr. At the time of Burr's occupancy this was farmland and pretty far uptown as New York City went.

The estate's stables were a typical early 19th century three-storied building but barely recognizable as such when the proprietors of the Café Bizarre remodeled the structure and decorated the place, both inside and out, à la weird décor.

The owner's wife had unusual experiences here. One early morning, after she had locked up for the night, she remembered something inside and had to re-enter the empty building. She had the creepy feeling that she was not alone and peered into the dark recesses of the café.

A male apparition with folded arms stood tall in the shadows and with piercing black eyes stared at her. He sported a ruffled shirt – a fashion statement not known in our time. She called out to him, but he was stoic. He didn't move an inch – just stood there and stared. She rushed out never looking back!

When the establishment changed to Quantum Leap Café, the haunting activity continued. Several employees and patrons observed the same male ghost in a puffy shirt and piercing black eyes.

The arrogant apparition is considered to be the specter of the American statesman Aaron Burr.

Burr's achievements include rising to the office of Vice-President but he is remembered more for his dastardly deeds that for his accomplishments. Burr's duel with Alexander Hamilton resulted in Hamilton's death; his imperialistic schemes resulted in charges of treason. Burr was acquitted on both counts, but his reputation was ruined. Maybe that's why he cannot rest.

Aaron Burr was interred at Princeton Cemetery alongside his father, a former Princeton president, but it appears that Burr prefers a metropolitan afterlife. Comparing the city's ghostly census, Burr's unearthly appearances outnumber all others.

Locked out of his long gone stables, you may see Burr's brooding wraith standing on the corner of W. 3rd and Sullivan Streets looking very lost.

FRANCIS HOUSE
27 Jane Street

Nineteen-year-old Alexander Hamilton caught the attention of his commander when stationed in Harlem Heights. General George Washington promptly promoted Hamilton to his aide-de-camp.

Hamilton's ascent to power had begun, along with his bitter rivalry with Aaron Burr. Hamilton foiled both Aaron Burr's attempt to become president of the United States in 1800 and his run for governor of New York four years later.

The two men's intense hatred for each other reached its peak on July 11, 1804, when they faced off in a pistol duel. Hamilton was wounded and taken to his physician at 27 Jane Street but Dr. John Francis was unable to help the mortally injured statesman. Hamilton died at home (80 Jane Street).

Before the Francis House was razed tenants were certain the place was haunted. Indistinct voices were heard, doors opened and closed on their own, and shadowy figures moved about. One woman stated that Hamilton himself materialized dressed in period clothing. He was hurrying about apparently in a rush to get somewhere quick.

RIVERVIEW HOTEL
113 Jane Street

The Institute of the Seaman's Friend was founded in Greenwich Village as a boarding house for able-bodied seamen. The building now houses the Riverview Hotel and the adjacent ballroom is home to the Jane Street Theater

According to *Haunted Holidays* (Jane Foreman, Editor), in April 1912, when the survivors of the *Titanic* disembarked from their rescue ship *Carpathia,* they found refuge at the sailor's lodging.

Throughout the night it seemed as if the terror experienced within the ill-fated ship during her last moments was being played out in the hallways. Occupants heard terrible screams and sobs outside their rooms. The manager and boarders tried to find the source of the awful sounds but there was no explanation – other than the spirits of those who had drowned in the icy Atlantic.

Another odd incident was that the elevator moved between the floors of its own accord.

It seemed to those that lived to tell the tale that some on the doomed ship had attached themselves to the living.

CHERRY LANE THEATRE
38 Commerce Street

The building that houses the Cherry Lane Theatre was functioning as a brewery in 1836 and the structure also served for a time as a tobacco warehouse and a box factory.

In 1924, writer Edna St. Vincent Millay along with other local artists formed an experimental theater group and converted the deserted space into the Cherry Lane Playhouse.

According to *Greenwich Village and How it Got That Way*, the theater's founders wanted a "cheery" name for their playhouse, opposed to London's Drury Lane Theatre, more commonly called "Dreary Lane." A reporter mistook the word "cheery" for "cherry" and the name stuck. Contrary to a long held belief, no cherry trees ever graced Commerce Street.

Another corollary to the Drury Lane Theatre, notorious for its hauntings, is that the Cherry Lane Theatre is also home to a number of ghosts.

Three spirits feature prominently among the theater's legends. What *is* unusual is that no one

*Appearing nightly at the diminutive Cherry Lane Theatre:
several unknown ghosts.*

can figure out who they are although there's plenty of opinion as to who they might be.

Many believe the resident ghosts are Aaron Burr or Thomas Paine since both men lived in the area. Some theorize that one is Washington Irving a frequent visitor to the neighborhood – his sister lived down the lane at 11 Commerce Street.

When the specters put in an appearance their cloudy forms float near the top of the staircase, or they perform their phantom pantomime in the hallway near the dressing rooms.

Was Edna St. Vincent Millay inspired by a personal encounter in her garden when she penned her 1917 poem, "The Little Ghost?"

If your dish shatters, or if your chair moves without help of human hand, you're probably dining at One If By Land.

ONE IF BY LAND, TWO IF BY SEA
17 Barrow Street

This romantic restaurant where marriage proposals are an almost daily occurrence once housed Aaron Burr's horse-drawn carriages and coaches. Where soft piano music permeates the atmosphere, sometimes dishes crash and are said to be an angry manifestation of Burr's spirit. The menace also likes to pull the chairs out from under diners.

But the cantankerous Burr is not the only presence known to haunt the eating-place.

The year after his infamous duel that ruined his political career, Burr's daughter, Theodosia, was lost at sea. Theodosia Burr Alston was on her way to visit her father when her ship disappeared off the North Carolina coast. Burr was extremely close to Theo and he never recovered from her loss. It's a comfort to know that at least the pair can be together in a place where other couples share tender moments.

Theo's spirit is as prankish as her father's. She is known to remove women's earrings. On occasion her specter materializes along with two other unidentified turn of the century spooks.

This Leroy Street house, a working class version of the Old Merchant's House, harbors the spirit of Elsbeth, caught in the act with a married man and then murdered by his irate wife. Is it guilt that keeps the girl's ghost attached to the spot?

OLD MERCHANT'S HOUSE
29 East 4th Street

The fascinating history of the Old Merchant's House is tarnished with sadness. Two spinster sisters, Gertrude and Sarah Tredwell, lived in the well-to-do home long after their tyrannical father died. The eccentric pair became more and more withdrawn and left the house only under the cover of night to buy food and other necessities.

Their story begins in 1835 when "uptown" meant 14th Street and where wealthy New Yorkers moved to escape crowded lower Manhattan. The neighborhood's well-to-do dwellings showcased the residents' wealth.

Considered one of the finest examples of Greek Revival architecture in the nation, the Merchant's House is a city landmark and a unique survivor of 19th century New York.

The decorative five-story brownstone was the Tredwell family home for a century. Seabury Tredwell, a stern and hard man, made his fortune in the hardware business. His wife Eliza bore him six children – four daughters and two sons. The oldest girls married well, the sons never really amounted to anything, and the youngest girls led a cold and loveless existence thanks to their cruel father.

Gertrude met the love of her life Lewis Walton, a medical student. Seabury took exception to the young man's status and was convinced the suitor was only after his sumptuous fortune. Another issue was that the young man was Catholic. Seabury was a dyed-in-the-wool Anglican. This unfortunate combination of circumstances made the man an ineligible match for his daughter. Gertrude was heart-broken. (Henry James' *Washington Square* is based on Gertrude's life.)

Seabury was so feared that Sarah committed suicide rather than face her father's wrath when she found out she was pregnant.

Another version of Sarah's story is that when she gave birth, her father paid a house servant to snuff out the baby's life in the house's secret tunnel, and within earshot of the new mother. Totally devastated and depressed, Sarah walked along the East River day and night. She eventually caught pneumonia and perished.

Either way, Sarah's death was by Seabury's hand. He died in 1865.

For many years, Gertrude lived in the house alone and oblivious to the changes in the world and within her own vicinity. She existed in the old house and never made any changes. She died in 1933 at the age of ninety-three.

The seven level house was a treasure trove furnished completely in 19th century fashion. All the family possessions - china, clothing, books, paintings, furniture, glassware, memorabilia, all left behind - an incomparable bequest.

Soon after Gertrude's death, the Historical Landmarks Society turned the Tredwell home into a museum. As caretakers and docents carefully sorted through the belongings and cataloged the items, they had the sensation that they were not alone.

A volunteer looked up from her work one day to see a female figure in a brown dress hovering on the nearby staircase and watching her. When the woman looked up again, the phantom was gone. The worker was certain it was Miss Gertrude observing the goings on in her house.

Reportedly another favored spot for Gertrude's ghost to materialize is in the parlor near the fireplace. When photographs taken in the house are developed they reveal strange and unexplainable anomalies, particularly those snapped in front of the hearth.

Many visitors catch a chill in Gertrude's bedroom. Museum staff will sometimes find the depression of a body on Gertrude's bed as if someone had slept in it the night before.

Other active areas in the old home include the kitchen and ground floor at the rear of the house. Over the last thirty years, a large number and variety of witnesses including journalists and psychic researchers have reported Gertrude's ghost.

Visitors have seen her figure "gliding" across floors and up the stairs and hearing her sighs and moans. Most uncanny is the piano music that filters through the historic home when no earthly being is seen sitting at Gertrude's favorite instrument.

When the love of her life was denied, she shut herself off from the world. Sadly, she shut herself in and lived in her own world. She still won't venture forth – not even to the great beyond.

ASTOR LIBRARY
425 Lafayette Street

John Jacob Astor built the first wing of his namesake library in 1853 long before the extraordinary Round Arched Style building housed the Joseph Papp Theater.

Six years later, in 1859, Washington Irving, who had died months earlier, was seen sitting amid the stacks, reading and writing, just as he often did when he was alive. Irving's dear friend, Dr. J. G. Cogswell, who had attended the man's funeral, collapsed at the sight of the specter.

Embarrassed to share the sighting he told no one. A few nights later, Cogswell again encountered Irving. As he approached his old crony, the being faded leaving a few cloudy patches of matter. The book Irving's ghost was holding crashed to the floor!

In due time Cogswell told selected friends of his unearthly experience. They advised him to get some rest, spend a couple of days in the country - the fresh air would do him good.

Eventually more and more library users witnessed the old specter who was also one of the library's founders. Oddly enough, Irving's nephew

Washington Irving's apparition appeared amid the stacks at the library he helped to found.

Pierre reported that Irving was also putting in post-mortem appearances at his Tarrytown home, *Sunnyside*.

One evening, while Pierre was sitting in the living room with his two daughters, Irving walked passed them, as plain as day, and entered his study.

Some theorized that the author stayed behind to complete an unfinished work; others felt it was just like Irving to pull pranks and that he was continuing his antics from beyond the grave.

Although Irving claimed he didn't believe in an afterlife, his scary tale *The Legend of Sleepy Hollow* abounded with haunted woods and a frightening headless horseman. Ironically, the author of America's first fictitious ghost story became the subject of New York's first *true* ghost story.

Since Irving was the first American author to be recognized internationally, the sightings of his ghost at the Astor Library, which lasted for decades, were widely publicized around the world.

Elizabeth Bullock's ghost in this Bank Street townhouse made its presence known one hundred years after her death.

BANK STREET

At the turn of the 18th century, Greenwich Village was a country hamlet dotted with elegant estates including Aaron Burr's Richmond Hill, which stood on the Hudson below present day Fourteenth Street.

When yellow fever broke out downtown, the Bank of New York moved its operations from Wall Street to a quiet country lane in the rural village. The epidemic brought a building boom to Bank Street.

Elizabeth Bullock's ghost would reside in one of those red brick town homes one hundred years later.

One day as she stepped off a bus, a speeding car killed her. There would be no resting in peace for her, however. Elizabeth's Protestant husband and Catholic parents began to argue over her dead body and where it would be buried.

Her husband ordered the body cremated and picked up her ashes early in the morning the next day. Her remains were sealed in a metal can labeled with her name and date of death. As he approached his home, he spotted his burly brothers-in-law on their way to save their sister's body from eternal damnation. The husband eluded them and ducked into a boarding house on Bank Street that was being renovated. He climbed to the second floor and stuck the can of ashes up onto an exposed beam.

In 1957 when new owners were restoring the boarding house to its original single family design, they regularly heard footsteps going up the stairway and walking across the second floor, followed by a light tapping sound. This occurred during daylight hours. The inexplicable sounds didn't bother them – they were happy to share their space with an invisible housemate.

One day as a workman hammered, plaster came down along with the can of Elizabeth's ashes. Realizing this might well be the cause of their haunting, they contacted parapsychologist Hans Holzer to conduct a séance.

To no avail, Elizabeth herself was not of any help in determining where she should be buried. She would not be comfortable with her husband in the Protestant cemetery nor did she want to be with her parents in the Catholic burial ground.

The owners of 11 Bank Street solved the problem themselves by burying Elizabeth's ashes in their garden with a non-sectarian cross to mark the spot. The noises ceased and were never heard again. At last, Elizabeth rests in peace.

THE WAVERLY INN
16 Bank Street

Many patrons at this legendary restaurant have witnessed the specter of a man in 19th century attire.

The Waverly Inn is the perfect place for a haunting…built in 1844 as a tavern, it also operated for a time as a bordello and a carriage house. When it opened as a teahouse in the 1920s, poet Robert Frost was a regular.

Mysterious noises continue to resound throughout the classic building but the most mystifying incident of all was the 1996 fire.

An investigation could not determine the cause or of the blaze or why Room 16 was untouched by the flames. The *only* explanation truly seemed to be an unbelievable one but there was no other – it must have been the resident ghost.

Room 16 was where the spirit of the male malingerer usually manifested.

Having vented his anger through the incendiary action, the fire-raising wraith made sure he fire proofed his own turf!

"Peg Leg Pete," interred at St. Mark's, refuses to rest – he continues to patrol his beloved "Bouwerie."

ST. MARK'S CHURCH IN THE BOWERY
131 East 10th at 2nd Avenue

Born in the Netherlands around 1592, Peter Stuyvesant began his career with the Dutch West India Company in 1632. During an expedition he severely injured his right leg, which led to its amputation. In 1645, he arrived in New Amsterdam (later New York City) as director general.

There is no delicate way of saying it - "Peg leg Pete" was a tyrant. After he was forced to surrender to the British, he spent the rest of his days on his farm, the "Bouwerie," from which New York City's "Bowery" takes its name.

Peter Stuyvesant's mansion was located on present day Stuyvesant Street. In 1672, he erected the first church where St. Mark's stands today. One hundred years later a new church was erected on the land donated by Peter's great-great grandson. That's when the hauntings began.

The 1799 Catholic Church is built on land of historic proportions, and not surprisingly remains a sanctuary for a number of ghosts. Some say the apparition of a female parishioner wanders the center aisle. The spirit of a second woman who wears a wide

Peter Stuyvesant's apparition ambles down his namesake street toward Cooper Square.

skirt has been witnessed standing near the rear of the church. A wispy white form has been known to hover in the balcony next to the organ.

Not surprisingly the apparition of a ghostly man with a wooden leg and walking stick is none other than Peter Stuyvesant himself.

Stuyvesant died in 1672 at the remarkable age of eighty and was buried in the family vault. Soon after he passed away, it quickly spread his ghost was frequently seen ambling about his former property.

Even today, Bowery residents, tourists, and the homeless, claim to encounter the phantom man tottering along the sidewalks of the Bowery, which was originally the road to his farm. The ghost, clad in distinctive vintage garb, is most often spotted limping along Stuyvesant Avenue toward Cooper Square.

Sometimes his specter is not seen but heard. One hundred years after his death the bells of the ancient church began to peal in the dead of night for no reason. Yet the parishioners felt certain they knew who the invisible culprit was; Peter Stuyvesant continued to wreck havoc with people even after death. At times, the disembodied *thudding* sound of his peg leg and walking stick in the sacred nave was enough to give churchgoers the willies!

The portal to the "Twain House" – a place said to be packed with ghosts.

MARK TWAIN HOUSE
14 West 10th Street

Mark Twain had an interest in ghosts and included them in a short story or two. Possibly it was his tenancy at 14 West 10th Street that stimulated his fascination.

Supposedly the ghosts of the twenty-two people who have died there haunt this Victorian apartment house. Some say Twain haunts the building's stairwell, but the consensus is that the ghosts of murdered children haunt the place.

Author Dennis William Hauck writes in *Haunted Places*, that prior to World War II, immigrants tortured their child by making the youngster walk around in circles for hours while tied to a rope looped over the top of a chair. The young child eventually succumbed to starvation.

The house seems to exude a peculiar energy and a dark and brooding presence pervades the place and perhaps penetrates the people living within its walls.

Jan Bryant Bartell was a former tenant, and Twain enthusiast, who wrote a book about her experiences with the building's ghosts, entitled *Spindrift*.

During her ten years in the apartment, Bartell exhaustingly chronicled all of the inexplicable events that transpired in her home.

From the moment the actress/writer moved in to her top-floor apartment, the sound of disembodied footsteps began. Nobody was ever seen but the footsteps echoed in the hall during the day when no one else was at home in the building. When the steps seemed to have reached their destination a sort of rustling sound was heard as if someone rushed to greet them.

A cleaning woman claimed to have witnessed a woman in white swish through the smallest room. Bartell slept in this room and invariably would awaken between 2:30 - 3:00 AM sensing someone standing beside her bed. Frequently she felt a feathery touch on her face and arms.

In the largest room a huge black shadow crossed the wall and the air was perfumed with a fragrance unfamiliar to Bartell or anyone else she knew.

Bartell and the maid weren't the only ones to be spooked by the odd goings on. Both her dogs would stare into space as if looking at something only they could discern. Sometimes the canines appeared to be stalking an unseen prey.

Another time, a delivery boy appeared at the door pale with fright and asked Bartell if the house was haunted. When asked why he replied that *something had followed him up the staircase!*

Friends visiting the apartment would be alone in a room and when they felt the presence of another person enter they would turn around expecting Jan, but *nobody was there!* Bartell had these same feelings that someone was behind her in the kitchen, but no one ever was. These experiences were frightening.

Bartell battled self-doubt but others' encounters confirmed her suspicions that she was not crazy nor was she alone in the apartment. The actress' nerves were frayed and her good health began to deteriorate.

Often a loud crashing noise resounded as if something had been dropped, but nothing was ever found broken.

What was discovered once was a wrinkled grape perfectly centered on an empty plate in the kitchen when there were no grapes in the house

Bartell's residence was formerly the servants' quarters. A lot of structural changes had occurred within the dwelling over the years, converting the 19th century mansion into an apartment building.

Some speculated that the ghosts, unfamiliar with the newly configured space, were trapped and couldn't fathom how to get out.

Admittedly Bartell knew she had psychic capabilities, but these disturbing happenings would be more than enough to drive a person to question their sanity.

Bartell passed away shortly after moving out. Some theorize it was suicide; her family asserts that her death was due to natural causes. Her book, *Spindrift,* was published posthumously in 1974.

On November 5, 1987, Joel Steinberg resided in a third-floor apartment here and murdered his adopted seven-year-old daughter, Lisa, by beating her to death.

This most recent horror only adds to the house's already macabre reputation,

JOHN LA FARGE RESIDENCE
45 West 10th Street

The Episcopalian Church Of The Ascension, at 5th Avenue and West 10th Street, commissioned painter and stained glass artist John La Farge, to create a mural. He completed the work in 1888.

At the very moment LaFarge died in 1910, the mural fell from its moorings in the church. Some claimed it was the heavy lead paint that caused it to fall and posthumously accused LaFarge of an improper design for the painting's scaffolding.

That's when the sightings of LaFarge's ghost were reported at the church and in his 10th Street studio building. The "10th Street Studio Building," was a Neo-Greco affair modeled after a studio in Paris. The building housed Hudson River School artists in its twenty-five studios.

Several tenants reported encounters with LaFarge's ghost who, when seen, was rummaging through their dresser drawers.

It is widely held that LaFarge was searching for his original plans for the scaffolding in an effort to clear his name. LaFarge's phantom has kept out of sight for the past forty years.

*Some have seen John LaFarge's phantom admiring his work
in the Church of the Ascension.*

GAY STREET GHOST
12 Gay Street

In 1881, Mayor James J. Walker was born in Greenwich Village and elected to the city's highest office in 1925. Considered the "toast of the town," Walker left the governance of the city to his aides while much of his honor's time was spent welcoming celebrities and riding in parades.

The flamboyant former mayor owned the property at 12 Gay Street and leased the place to a young woman whom he "admired."

A procession of disembodied footsteps moving up and down the stairway in this tiny 1800 townhouse has been audible to many residents. When the noise is investigated, *no body is there!* Psychic mediums discerned a gambling den and opium smokers in the rooms above the busy stairway.

A male apparition in evening dress and opera cape has appeared many times inside and in front of the abode. Could this debonair ghost, who smiles politely, then disappears, be the spiritual remains of the colorful Mayor?

*Who's the dandy denizen inside former
Mayor Jimmy Walker's townhouse?*

Former resident and author of *The Shadow*, Walter Gibson, felt the spirits were psychic impressions he left behind when he wrote the mystery series here in the late 1940s. Gibson fantasized that his characters lived with him and he considered them real people.

The author's crime fighting hero, Lamont Cranston often wore a cape and top hat. Does Cranston live on and walk the tangled Greenwich Village streets?

Another telltale sign of a ghostly presence is the strong scent of violets. Even pet dogs detect the scent and sniff the air to determine the source. They wag their tails in response to the invisible visitor.

*The historic White Horse Tavern where the wraith
of Dylan Thomas still reigns.*

WHITE HORSE TAVERN
567 Hudson Street
(At West 11th Street)

This creaky old landmark tavern built in 1880 has witnessed a lot of history from its days as a tumultuous sailors' hangout to a speakeasy and hangout for literary bohemians during Greenwich Village's heyday.

Bob Dylan was a regular in the 1960s and poet Dylan Thomas was said to have drunk himself to death here. Supposedly his last words were, "I've had 19 straight whiskies. I believe that's the record." He died in the hospital later that night.

The tavern has dedicated a room to Thomas complete with his portraits. Some feel the writer's spirit continues to make his presence known by rotating his favorite table and rattling glasses just as he did when he was alive.

Is the invisible wraith demanding a 20th jigger?

The table where proprietor Henrietta Chumley downed her final manhattan and drew her last breath.

CHUMLEY'S
86 Bedford Street

Chumley's, the only speakeasy left in the nation, has a phantom proprietor who runs the establishment from beyond the grave.

This warm and cozy restaurant is a veritable institution. Chumley's patronage boasts a long list of distinguished writers including John Steinbeck, J.D. Salinger, Ernest Hemingway, and Edna Ferber. Some claim that Robert F. Kennedy would hunker down at a corner table and pen his inspired speeches.

In 1928 artist, writer, and soldier-of-fortune Lee Chumley bought the building and converted the blacksmith shop into a tavern. The forge was transformed into the fireplace. Chumley's moody ambience drew its clientele by word-of-mouth. No sign marked its door, not then, not now.

The Greenwich Village landmark attracted a literary crowd and Chumley started the tradition of bordering the walls with the dust covers of his writer/patrons' latest book. The custom continues to this day and the original vintage covers are still visible and intact.

After Chumley left this world for the next, many were surprised when *Mrs.* Henrietta Chumley showed up and ran the establishment. Every night she reigned over her domain from her favorite spot next to the fireplace, slugging down manhattans and playing solitaire until she passed out over the cards spread out on the corner table.

One night at closing as the bartenders finished their clean up, a waiter went to rouse the boss so she could begin her stagger home. Unfortunately, Henrietta's lifeless body had been out cold for the better part of the evening.

A crackling fire continued to warm the regulars when the cold winds blustered, but the new owners soon found out that they had a silent partner whose invisible presence left them chilly and whose antics spoke volumes and gave them the willies!

They thought that installing a video game was a good idea to enhance business. The electronic game didn't work right from the start. Then the jukebox went on the fritz. When the video game was removed, the jukebox went back to normal. No explanation was ever found. The management just figured that Henrietta maintained a death grip on the operation and wanted to keep the *status quo.*

P.S. The video game worked fine for its new owner!

OLD ST. PATRICK'S CATHEDRAL
263 Mulberry Street

Pierre Toussaint is on the verge of becoming North America's first African American saint. Pope John Paul II declared this remarkable man "venerable," the first step toward sainthood.

When New York City was our fledging nation's capital, 18th century Haiti was a cultural center and the wealthiest colony in the world. When the French Revolution incited unrest and upheaval on the island nation in 1793, wealthy plantation owner Jean Bérard fled to Manhattan with his family and entourage of slaves.

With three fashionable young women in his family, Bérard apprenticed his educated slave Pierre Toussaint to a local hairdresser.

When Bérard died, Toussaint, being the only male, supported the eight-member household with wages earned as a society hairdresser. Toussaint worked a 16-hour day, walking from house to house in a twelve-block radius, coifing the curls of the rich and famous. Even George Washington had his locks tended by the talented man.

*Moved from his Mulberry Street resting place to uptown, the
saintly Pierre Toussaint seems to prefer his former digs.*

This is only one example of his many humanitarian acts. He and his wife Juliette (he feverishly saved to purchase her freedom) nursed the sick, even the forsaken plague victims, raised orphans and found them jobs, and sheltered refugees.

Toussaint contributed financially to the construction of Old St. Patrick's Cathedral, the city's oldest Catholic Church. He and his family were buried in the cemetery there, their weather worn headstone discovered in 1938.

Referred to as "St. Pierre" when alive, devotees have attributed miracles to the virtuous man. The Catholic Church has recognized his work from beyond the grave and is well underway toward truly anointing him a saint.

Cardinal O'Connor had Toussaint's remains exhumed and moved to the uptown St. Patrick's Cathedral. It seems, however, that the former slave prefers his more humble digs.

On her deathbed, Madame Bèrard freed Toussaint, but his spirit seems to have remained earthbound.

Many tell of sightings of Toussaint's shade traipsing about the tombstones in Old Saint Patrick's ancient graveyard.

CHARLES STREET SPECTER

British fashion designer Barrie Gaunt was a tenant in a ground floor apartment here in the 1960s and shared his space with a sad spirit for years. Where and whenever he moved in the apartment, a vapor seemed to follow him (talk about being in a fog!) The sound of audible breathing also bothered Barrie.

Some overnight guests complained that unseen hands had violently pushed them awake. For no known reason, one woman was overcome with grief while visiting Gaunt.

During a 1964 investigation conducted by the able ghost-busting duo of parapsychologist Hans Holzer and psychic medium/witch Sybil Leek, a spirit by the name of Mary Elizabeth Boyd was contacted. The entity adamantly claimed title to the property and also shared that she had died in the house in 1886 while looking for the deed.

According to official records, a woman named Boyd did at that time live in the house with her father. Apparently she was still living there eighty years after her death deeply disturbed by that dastardly, and misplaced, deed.

SONNENBERG MANSION
19 Irving Place

Corporate public relations consultant Benjamin Sonnenberg was once the proud owner of the grand 19th century Gramercy Park mansion. The legendary publicist poured his heart and soul into refurbishing the building and decorating the interior with authentic period furnishings.

At his death it was his wish to be buried on the grounds. That of course was illegal. According to the information in Hans Holzer's *Travel Guide to Haunted Places*, however, Sonnenberg's remains *did* find their way onto the property.

Strangely enough, it is not Sonnenberg's specter that has been spotted at the site.

The caretakers living in the former servants' quarters, were startled at the sight of a woman on the stairs who quickly vanished before their eyes. They also heard footsteps and doors open and close *when no body was in the building!*

Perhaps the female phantom was one of Ben's lady friends who dropped by to pay her respects.

SMUGGLER'S GHOST

One of the most gruesome ghost tales revolves around Magda Hamilton a police informant who busted an international smuggling ring operating out of 20 Mott Street in the 1870s.

Hamilton's testimony indicted the dwarfish Eileen Ridley, also known as Fanchon Moncaré.

Moncaré had perfected her technique of posing as the ward of her partner, Ada Danworth, and carrying a china doll stuffed with a ¼ million dollars worth of diamonds right through customs.

When it came time to divide the loot at the lair of the ring's leader Wing Hong Tow, Moncaré lost her little girl act and showed her true character – a vile, conniving crook. Danforth hated this scene and many times had to leave the room. The demeanor of her ominous partner was frightening.

Initially, Magda Hamilton worked together with Moncaré on a scheme to rob a Chicago millionaire. The successful caper made Magda an accepted member of the mob. All was well with the pair until Moncaré swindled Magda. This betrayal ended their association, but unwittingly, Moncaré had met her match. Magda didn't like being doubled crossed.

Things turned sour for the Moncaré/Danforth team during a job in France. The plan was to rip off a wealthy and eccentric Frenchman who wore, and carried on his person, all his expensive jewelry. When their male accomplice walloped the old man on the head to knock him out, the blow was fatal.

Robbery was one thing, but no way were the two women going to be implicated in murder. They cut short their stay and hot tailed it home.

As the ship pulled into the New York port, the atmosphere was tense. Investigators flanked the customs officers. At first it seemed as if Moncaré's performance had passed scrutiny, but as she walked down the ramp she was nabbed by police and fought like a tiger. A veiled woman standing off to the side smiled under her cover.

Newspapers reported the sensational trial and stated that a masked woman had secretly informed police of the smuggling operation; its tentacles reached into Boss Tweed's administration.

The two women were convicted. Moncaré got a life sentence, Danforth, twenty years.

Moncaré and Danforth had lived together in a beautiful mansion on Staten Island. A decorative widow's walk with a view of New York harbor graced the top of the structure. To add insult to injury, when Magda betrayed her cohorts, she and her husband moved into the lavish home.

The years passed and Danforth was freed. She went on to set up a women's boutique in the city.

Moncaré died while imprisoned.

Magda's husband eventually left her in search of gold in California.

One night Magda awoke with a start. She was certain that someone was in her bedroom. An old dwarfish woman emerged from the shadows and held a china doll like a dagger. Magda tried to scream but her cries were muffled as the doll was shoved down her throat.

The coroner ruled her death suffocation. No one was ever indicted for the crime.

For years, realtors complained about how difficult it was to keep tenants in the house. Some stayed a few months; some didn't make it through a full week.

Before the house was razed, people in the neighborhood heard awful screams emanating from the old place. Boaters reported to the harbor authorities that they often spied a smallish woman on the widow's walk of the old house. They said she seemed to be holding a doll dripping with blood...

BARKER HOUSE
East 26th Street

Alanda Hanna Barker and her two sisters lived in their 26th Street house for over fifty years. When the American Society for Psychical Research (ASPR) investigated the 1859 brownstone, they concluded that indeed the place was haunted - *very* haunted.

When the building was being renovated in 1978, strange things began to happen. Strains of classical music often filtered throughout the house, objects moved of their own accord, and the strong scent of lavender was suffocating.

When a full-bodied apparition of a young girl manifested, the new owners rushed to call in the ghost busters - ASPR.

ASPR's conclusions brought no relief. Counted among the ghostly residents in the apartment were a tall, thin man in Revolutionary War garb, a male boat builder in the backyard, a grieving woman dressed in mourning clothes, a bawdy female, and the ghost of a fluffy dog.

Neighbors even reported that phantom prostitutes walked the streets in front of the former bordello.

SUGAR HOUSE PRISON
Police Plaza

Across from City Hall, remnants of the Rhinelander Sugar Warehouse are set into the wall of the modern 11-story Rhinelander Building. A barred window and some old Dutch bricks memorialize the American Revolution's prisoners of war.

During the occupation of New York by the British (1776-1783) the sugar warehouse was used as a jail. The lockup was notorious for its cruel and inhuman treatment of prisoners. Hundreds died of starvation and disease inside the filthy stockade. The sadistic Provost Marshall William Cunningham presided over the prisons and took pleasure in executing American patriots, including Nathan Hale.

For a hundred years before the deserted warehouse was leveled in 1875, tales were told of anguished phantom faces peering out from behind the barred windows. Wraithlike hands reached out to passersby beseeching them to help. In the dead of night, no one in their right mind went near the haunted spot.

226 FIFTH AVENUE

The rental ad for the studio apartment read:

"Attic dark room with a ghost."

Many times tenants reported seeing the green glowing ghost of Confederate General Samuel Edward McGowan swinging from the attic rafters.

McGowan was strangled to death in this apartment by his mistress' boyfriend who staged the murder to look like a suicide by hanging the deceased Southerner from the beams.

The Confederate War hero once fought a duel over a woman and had been injured seven times in battle. Those who knew McGowan always felt that "his women would be the death of him."

When his body was returned to South Carolina for burial, his 1873 obituary read that he had died at home with friends and family after a brief but painful illness.

Since the green glowing ghost persisted in its appearances, many felt the victim wanted the truth told about his murder and the perpetrator brought to justice.

The specters of those who leapt to their death from the landmark structure are rumored to still be among the living on the great building's observation deck.

EMPIRE STATE BUILDING
350 Fifth Avenue at 34ᵗʰ Street

The Empire State Building soars more than a ¼ mile into the Manhattan sky offering visitors breathtaking views from its two observatories. On a clear day visitors can see up to 80 miles.

Constructed in 1931, this National Historic Landmark, famous for its Art Deco architecture, has been a favored destination for millions of people from all over the world who are proud to boast that they have been to the top of the celebrated building.

Years before the protective barriers were raised higher, the famed skyscraper was the scene of many dramatic suicides. Eagle-eyed guards provide further protection for any potential jumpers.

The ghosts of those who nose-dived to their death are said to haunt the observation deck especially at night. The sightings and escapades of a particular young female phantom are legendary. She is believed to have committed suicide by jumping from the deck after hearing that her fiancée was killed during World War II.

Those who tell the tale describe a full-bodied apparition of a woman wearing circa 1940s clothing, gloves and bright red lipstick. The 20+ year old seems lost in her own world and can be heard softly bemoaning her fate, uttering phrases like "My man died in the war," or, "We were going to be married," or "He died in Germany." The distraught specter then races to the barrier and somehow hurls herself over the top.

Some of those who have observed the frightful scene believe they are hallucinating due to the elevated atmosphere. Some women who have witnessed this horrifying act have rushed to the restroom to gain their composure only to encounter the strange woman applying her trademark red lipstick!

When asked how she did that "trick," the red-lipped woman stares into space and sadly replies, "We were childhood sweethearts, we were going to be married…"

Look around on the observation deck and maybe you'll catch a glimpse of the woman with ruby red lips in a vintage dress looking liked she stepped out of the forties. She probably did.

Some say that Samuel "Roxy" Rothafel has never left his Radio City Music Hall. Roxy's rakish revenant has been spotted roaming the aisles.

HAVOC HOUSE
428 West 44th Street

For seven years in the 1960s, stage and television actress June Havoc lived in the basement apartment of this 44th Street townhouse. At the rear of the Victorian apartment she continually heard a noise that sounded like tap dancing. Havoc thought it was the steam pipes.

Workers were called in to find the problem and fix it but nothing was amiss. There was no explanation for the racket.

Enter specter sleuth Hans Holzer and British psychic medium Sybil Leek.

Leek made contact with the entity who was *desperately hungry and wanted some food!* Turns out the hungry one was a camp follower named Lucy Ryan still stuck in the year 1782. She was clamoring for attention because she was *starving.*

Subsequent tenants claimed they perceived the disembodied sound of someone looking through the kitchen cabinets as if an unseen ghost was rummaging for something to eat.

Those who experienced the ghost nicknamed her "Hungry Lucy."

BELASCO THEATRE
111 West 44th Street

On opening night in October 1907, the Stuyvesant Theatre was the most innovative playhouse in the world, thanks largely to producer David Belasco.

Belasco refurbished and redecorated the first-rate house preserving the Tiffany glass windows and hand painted murals. He wanted a stylish, grand showplace to showcase his elaborate productions. The vaudeville theater featured many advances - dimmer switches were used for the first time and a catwalk enabled stagehands to provide special effects.

Belasco eventually bought the Stuyvesant, renamed it after himself, and lived in the lavish upstairs suite, the scene of many celebrated parties.

After his death in 1931, the racket of revelry continued to resound from the upper quarters. Stagehands shivered when they heard the machinations of the private elevator gear up even though the creaky old lift hadn't worked in years.

Actors and theater personnel eagerly anticipated the sight of Belasco's specter in his private box every opening night. The impresario's phantom made every premier until the 1970s when for the first time

Eerie goings-on in the theatre that bears his name are attributed to the eccentric producer David Belasco.

in theater history, nudity was introduced on stage in the production of *Oh! Calcutta!*

Another hair-raising event was when Belasco's shade materialized in the alley near the stage door entrance. His full-bodied appearance donning a long robe and his characteristic rumpled white hair were dead giveaways.

It seems that Belasco has company with him in the theater's after life. A theatre worker stated very matter-of-factly, that the she had seen the apparition of a redheaded woman in a white negligee. She is thought to be the shade of a stripper who hung herself in the cellar. Her transparent form was sometimes seen dramatically descending a circular staircase.

Belasco's namesake theater is not his only haunt. The renowned showman's revenant also makes the scene at the New Victory Theater.

In 1902 Belasco leased the 42nd Street theatre from Oscar Hammerstein.

When the curtain falls on the final act and theatergoers file out, those last to leave feel an icy chill that they ascribe to Belasco - the long dead impresario's way of saying *"Good Night"* from the great beyond.

The lifetime dream of two Royal Air Force pilots was fulfilled when they paid a phantom visit to Times Square.

TIMES SQUARE

During World War II, Harvard University graduate Oswald Remsen, had an unnerving experience in the heart of the theater district at Broadway and 45th Street near Times Square.

According to Daniel Cohen's *The Ghosts of War*, while Remsen waited at the corner for the light to change, two men in Royal Air Force uniforms stopped next to him and looked at their watches. They seemed mesmerized with the surroundings and asked the Harvard man if this was Times Square. Remsen thought the question odd, but assured them that indeed this was the famous "crossroads of the world." Again, they checked their watches.

The three walked along in the same direction for quite some time and soon began to converse. The pilots were thrilled to be in such a delightful spot after their terrible ordeal in the war. After looking at their watches Remsen asked if they had an appointment. They didn't, so Remsen invited the pair to join him for dinner at the Harvard Club. They were delighted and accepted the invitation after they glanced at their watches.

The Englishmen praised the dinner, and were vague about sharing their wartime experiences, which Remsen felt was normal. What seemed odd however, was their abnormal clock watching. The men assured him they had nowhere to go.

At 11:55 PM, however, the two pilots abruptly stood up and thanked Remsen for a lovely evening. One of them exclaimed that it was the *strangest* evening that he had ever had and went on to explain to his host that just twenty-four hours earlier, *the Englishmen had been killed when their plane was shot down over Berlin.*

The two *phantom* pilots then proceeded to the exit and simply vanished.

PALACE THEATER
1564 Broadway and 47th Street

Martin Beck built the famous Palace Theater in 1912 and called it the "Valhalla of Vaudeville." All of the greatest stars played the Palace – Jack Benny, Irving Berlin, Sarah Bernhardt, Eddie Cantor, Judy Garland, Harry Houdini, and Sophie Tucker – Fanny Brice was the first to have her name in lights.

One of the most unforgettable acts was in the 1950s when tightrope walker Louis Borsalino fell to his death during a performance.

For years after the tragedy, stagehands saw the performer's specter backstage swinging from the dress-circle rim, according to *Haunted Places: The National Directory* (Dennis William Hauck).

Some hauntings are like a film loop; the tragedy plays itself over and over again. Those who've experienced the paranormal at the Palace swear they've heard the tightrope walker's terrified screams and observed the apparition of his falling body as Borsalino plummeted to his death.

A phantom tightrope walker plummets to his death over and over at the Palace Theater.

NEW AMSTERDAM THEATRE
214 West 42nd Street

The mysterious circumstance of Olive Thomas Pickford's death in 1920 was Hollywood's first scandal. The 26-year-old actress died in Paris after ingesting mercurial bichloride. To this day, the question remains - was it an accident or a suicide?

Olive's husband, actor Jack Pickford (brother of Mary Pickford) maintained that Olive had trouble sleeping after a night out on the town and mistakenly swallowed the wrong medication.

The young actress suffered greatly for five days; Pickford never left her side. When she succumbed, an autopsy was conducted and an inquiry ensued. The French coroner ruled her death an accident.

The loss of the beautiful and engaging woman, who had appeared in 23 silent films, devastated her many friends and admirers. She was laid to rest in a white gown trimmed with silver beads. Four thousand mourners attended her funeral held at St. Thomas Episcopal Church on Fifth Avenue. Her body was interred at Woodlawn Cemetery in the Bronx.

*The New Amsterdam Theatre where former Follies girl
Olive Thomas still puts in post-mortem appearances.*

Olive left her first husband for reasons of cruelty and decided to escape the dreary confines of her life in a small Pittsburgh town. She came to Harlem to live with relatives.

Her rise to fame and fortune began when she entered a modeling contest for the "most beautiful girl" in New York. Olive's Irish beauty won her the top honor, her photograph in the newspaper.

Olive's photo caught the attention of Florenz Ziegfeld who was in the business of selling the image of the American girl by showcasing young women in his *Follies* presented on the rooftop stage of the New Amsterdam Theater. Olive was a sensation performing as "Miss January," one of the "Nightie-night Girls."

Today, adjacent towering structures dwarf the vintage theatre and although questions linger about Olive's death, the source of the answer to her demise may lie in the place where Olive's career blossomed and where her spirit puts in post-mortem appearances.

When the New Amsterdam was renovated, workers saw Olive's ghostly image dressed in a white gown trimmed with silver beads. The apparition was holding a blue glass bottle, supposedly the vial that held the lethal poison that killed her.

CLINTON COURT
422-½ West 46th Street

A pirate known as the "Old Moor" was hanged for mutiny at the Bowery in the late 18th century. He was buried in the potter's field where Governor DeWitt Clinton built his carriage house a century later. An iron gate marks the threshold to the three-storied arched building.

Seemingly the angry sailor could not rest in peace. Clinton Court was first in his path on his nightly forays so the vengeful ghost began his haunt.

An English coachman's wife came upon his dark wraith. As she ran away in fright, she fell to her death down the stairs. She was pregnant at the time and her baby lived. The coachman's wife could not relinquish her nurturing nature and her apparition was commonly seen shadowing her baby girl.

Unbelievably, the little girl enjoyed playing "ghost" and would wrap a sheet around her. Running down the stairs one day she tripped over the tangled fabric and, like her mother, fell to her death. The ghostly girl continues her phantom play.

That's how the neighbors tell the tale of the three ghosts of Clinton Court.

IL BRUNELLO RESTAURANT
West 56th Street

Before this Italian restaurant came to be, the place was called DaVinci's and during that time something amazing occurred within, and on, its walls.

The establishment's proximity to Madison Avenue made it a convenient place to stop after work to wind down or drown one's sorrows.

Drinking diluted the career of a particular advertising executive who spent a lot of time at DaVinci's. Too much time. He eventually succumbed to alcoholism and committed suicide.

It seemed his spirit never left this place of spirits. Workers found empty martini glasses on the bar where the man always sat.

Most cryptic of all were the advertising blurbs found scribbled on the walls of his former haunt.

CENTRAL PARK

Successful banker Norden Van der Voort had it all – an exclusive home, plenty of money, and a beautiful wife. Descended from a prominent New Amsterdam family, more than anything else, Van der Voort wanted a son to bear his name.

After his second daughter was born, bad news followed – this would be their last child. Van der Voort was devastated and turned his back on his wife and daughters.

Norden settled in Rhinebeck and continued to shun his family and friends. It was rumored that he loved fast horses and fast women.

The daughters, Janet and Rosetta, seldom saw their father. Their mother kept them close, yet on occasion the girls enjoyed summers abroad. While still in their teens, the prodigal Van Der Voort died in a riding accident.

Janet and Rosetta were inseparable. Two years apart, many thought they were twins. Their favorite place in the entire world was Central Park. "We're New Yorkers through and through," their mantra.

The attractive girls were introduced to many potential suitors but Janet and Rosetta showed no interest. Together the Dutch debutantes had one love and one love only – ice skating. Their mother was miffed, but she spent little time worrying about the girls, she had her own agenda – to remarry.

So, Janet and Rosetta, dressed in the height of fashion spent hours on the ice in Central Park's 59th Street Lake. They skated all morning, lunched at Delmonico's, then back to the park to skate for the remainder of the day. The pair was obsessed but their skill on the ice was becoming legendary.

Spring, summer, autumn wore on them. They were irritable, they bickered. They spent the humid summers months away from the city in Cape May and seldom ventured from their isolated cottage.

Their mother passed and when the will was read the girls were shocked to learn they were nearly broke! Their lawyer counseled them to be frugal but one last fling was already in the planning.

Janet's 35th birthday party was a nighttime gala held in Central Park, of course. A full moon illuminated the magnificent feast set on long tables on the ice; fireworks lit up the sky and provided a magical setting, fires in iron baskets kept chills away. Anyone who could stand on skates attended. The event cost a fortune.

The girls were stunning, Janet wore dark purple velvet, carried an ermine barrel muff. Rosetta dazzled in green satin covered with a red velvet cut-away coat edged with gray squirrel. The spectacular was widely reported in the society pages.

The sisters lived out their lives mostly pining for winter. When they grew too old to skate, they rarely left the house and passed the time playing cards. Janet passed away in 1915 at sixty-five, Rosetta died of a broken heart three months later.

During World War I, some visitors, lured into Central Park by the full moon, watched two women on the ice – one was outfitted in purple velvet, the other red. The female skaters were admired for years – *they must be professionals,* thought the onlookers. Spectators watching the women during an early thaw came to realize that the performance they were watching was truly out of this world …*two phantom skaters floated above the ice* on the 59th Street Lake.

OLD METROPOLITAN OPERA HOUSE
Broadway between 39th and 40th Streets

New York City's *nouveau riche* built their own opera house on Broadway in 1883. They wanted a place were all of high society had the privilege of individual opera boxes, a luxury denied them at the old Academy of Music due to the limited number of box seats.

This new Metropolitan Opera House that they erected had three levels of thirty-six boxes, more than enough to accommodate the current millionaires. The new socialites now had a theater that met their caprices.

Another member of the audience with attitude was Madame Frances Alda, the wife of director Giulio Gatti-Casazza. For years after her death she continued to attend performances at the posh opera palace. Her robust revenant sat front and center and disparaged performers by slinging loud and rude remarks. She especially targeted the young sopranos.

The old Met stood until 1966 when a 14-story opera house was built in Lincoln Center. Apparently Madame Alda's apparition moved on when the opera house did.

MOUNT VERNON HOTEL MUSEUM
421 East 61st Street

Over a century ago when midtown Manhattan was still rural, William Stephens Smith and President John Adams' daughter Abigail purchased 23 acres on the Upper East Side and erected a grand estate, which they named Mount Vernon in honor of George Washington's Virginia home.

When the main house burned to the ground in 1826, the stone carriage house was converted into an elegant resort called the Mount Vernon Hotel.

Hotels and inns were popular stopovers for folks making the long trek to the city. In the early 1800s, places like the Mount Vernon Hotel were an escape and a place of peace and quiet.

In 1939, the Colonial Dames of America opened the house as a museum. Today the museum, formerly the Abigail Adams Smith Museum, evokes an Old World atmosphere.

It seems that Abigail still considers the spot the perfect setting for she is said to still walk the halls of her former home, her audible footsteps a telltale sign of her ghostly presence.

GARROWAY HOUSE
East 63rd Street

TV personality Dave Garroway was the premier host of the *Today* show in 1952. At the time he lived in a six-story residence on East 63rd Street.

According to Dennis Hauck's *The National Directory of Haunted Places,* the nights in the Garroway house were hard to endure due to the inexplicable events that transpired there.

An angry unseen entity tormented the family nightly by opening every single door in the dwelling. Locking the portals was to no avail.

Garroway was worried that the malicious presence would frighten his children, so in an effort to quell the ghostly antics, he contacted a psychic medium to help release the spirit that was distressing his family.

The psychic made contact with the culprit - the spirit of an irate old man. Despite her efforts to release him from his earthbound existence, and free the home from the pesky phantom, his capers continued until the Garroways moved out.

THE DAKOTA
Central Park West at 72nd Street

In 1884, Edward Clark, president of the Singer Sewing Machine Company, erected this eerily eclectic edifice so far removed from the heart of the city it might well have been in "the Dakotas."

Roman Polanski used the grand apartment building as the setting for his film *Rosemary's Baby*. That alone is a spooky qualification. But the dwelling holds a real haunted history.

During a 1965 renovation workers witnessed the specter of a small boy walk down a hallway and *through the wall* between two rooms. Not long after that a group of painters saw a little girl ghost in Victorian dress skipping down a corridor.

John Lennon was shot to death in the Dakota's entrance on December 8, 1980. Doormen and passersby have encountered the long-gone Lennon in front of his former haunt (and at the Strawberry Fields memorial in Central Park). On occasion the departed Beatle will flash the peace sign.

The Dakota's dead are removed through a gate on 73rd Street, and according to some this portal is a very haunted spot...

CATHEDRAL OF ST. JOHN THE DIVINE
1047 Amsterdam Avenue at 110th Street

If awards were given for ferreting out phantoms, prolific author and parapsychologist Hans Holzer would win top prize. For decades he has devoted his life to studying the spirit world, and through the use of psychic mediums, has helped to dislodge the dead from their earthbound existence.

In his guidebook *Haunted Travels,* Holzer shares the haunted tale of a former Dean of the largest cathedral in the world.

When Bishop James Pike was the resident Dean of the Episcopal Cathedral of St. John the Divine he often heard disembodied shuffling about his quarters, known as the Deanery, which is a smaller building alongside the cathedral.

Bishop Pike eventually learned that the restless spirit was presumably a former Dean, Bishop Greer. The deceased bishop was unable to rest in peace because of the loss of a pectoral cross, a valuable church relic. To this day the cross has not been recovered nor has Bishop Greer's ghost recovered from its loss.

MORRIS JUMEL MANSION
65 Jumel Terrace

Built around 1765 as a summer retreat for British Colonel Roger Morris and his wife Mary Philipse, this colonial mansion in Washington Heights is Manhattan's oldest house. The Morrises abandoned the structure at the outbreak of the Revolution and George Washington moved in making the grand home his headquarters.

In 1810, a rich French wine merchant Stephen Jumel, and his wife Eliza, bought the estate. When Stephen died some felt Eliza had a hand in his death.

Eliza then married 77-year-old Aaron Burr in 1833. Some say this was a marriage of convenience for Eliza - a way to legitimize her wealth and allow her entrée to higher social circles. A stormy marriage prevailed, however, and Eliza ultimately sued for divorce. This was granted on September 14, 1836, the very day Aaron Burr died.

After Burr's death Eliza was snubbed by New York society and lived as a recluse in the mansion until her death at 93. Some say she was insane.

The historic house remained an ancestral home until 1865. Fortunately, the City of New York had the foresight to purchase the estate in 1903.

The fully restored abode features nine period rooms and at least three fantastic phantoms.

Without surprise, the spirit of Eliza Jumel, the former fiery mistress of the manse, is said to wander through the house in a purple dress rapping on windows and walls.

The servants' quarters are frequented by the specter of a young maid who supposedly committed suicide by leaping out a window.

The third bona fide ghost is a Revolutionary War soldier who is the subject of a painting that hangs in the mansion. More than one visitor and docent have shared that the depicted soldier comes alive on occasion.

The most momentous event of all occurred in the 1970s when a group of boisterous schoolchildren arrived for a tour. They spotted a mysterious woman dressed in purple on the second floor balcony who told them to *"Shush!"*

When they entered the home they discovered that no one *alive* inside the house at the time fit the description of the scolding specter!

WORLD TRADE TOWERS

In the aftermath of the World Trade Center attack on September 11, 2001, it was widely reported that Lower East Side residents looking toward Ground Zero witnessed a light going straight up into the sky that actually looked like the Twin Towers.

People gathered on the sidewalk to stare at the amazing sight of what many were calling the "Ghost of the Towers."

Surprisingly, individuals who've encountered ghosts are not afraid – just the opposite, they find the experience comforting.

Such was the case of the ghostly light emanating from where the towers once stood.

"It's a thing of God," said one observer.

Dedicated to all those
whose lives were touched
by the events of
September 11, 2001.

RESOURCES

ARTICLES:

"Some See 'Ghost' of Towers at Night" by Mae M. Cheng (NEWSDAY, September 23, 2001).

BOOKS:

Ghosts in American Houses, by James Reynolds (Bonanza Books, 1956).

Ghosts I've Met by Hans Holzer (Bobbs-Merrill Publishing, 1984).

Ghostly Tales of Love & Revenge, by Daniel Cohen (G.P. Putnam's Sons, 1992).

The Ghosts of War, by Daniel Cohen (G.P. Putnam's Sons, 1990).

GHOSTS, True Encounters With the World Beyond, by Hans Holzer (Black Dog & Levanthal Press, 1991).

Greenwich Village and How It Got That Way, by Terry Miller (Crown Publishers, 1990).

Haunted History of Staten Island, by Lynda Lee Macken (Black Cat Press, 2000).

Haunted Holidays, by Laura Foreman, Editor (Discovery Communications, 1999).

Haunted Places, The National Directory, by Dennis William Hauck (Penguin Press, 1996).

New York City Ghost Stories, by Charles J. Adams III (Exeter House Books, 1996).

Spindrift: Spray from a Psychic Sea, by Jan Bryant Bartell (Hawthorne Books, 1974).

Travel Guide to Haunted Houses, by Hans Holzer (Black Dog & Levanthal Press, 1998).

WEBSITES:

"Cherry Lane Theatre History," (cherrylanetheatre.com)

"British Prison Wall Stands in Park Here" by John McNamara (correctionhistory.org)

The Belasco Theatre and The Dakota (nyu.edu/classes)

"Ghost Town," (metronewyork.com)

Ghostly Gotham (gonyc.about.com/travel)

"Ghoulies and Ghosties: The Bank Street Ghost," by Doris Lane (themestream.com)

"Gotham's Ghosts," by Partha Banerjee and Joon-Nie Lau (nyc24.com/2000/issue03)

Morris-Jumel Mansion (preserve.org)

"Pierre Toussaint, a slave, society hairdresser, philanthropist, may become nation's first black saint" by Arthur Jones (National Catholic Reporter Online (natcath.com))

Other books by

Lynda Lee Macken

HAUNTED HISTORY OF STATEN ISLAND
ADIRONDACK GHOSTS
GHOSTS OF THE GARDEN STATE
HAUNTED SALEM & BEYOND
HAUNTED CAPE MAY

For purchasing information contact:

BLACK CAT PRESS
Post Office Box 1218
Forked River, New Jersey 08731

Email
llmacken@hotmail.com

DATE DUE ON LINE 11/02	
JAN 0 2 2003	
FEB 2 0 2003	
FEB 0 6 2003	
MAR 0 9 2006 (ILL)	

GAYLORD   PRINTED IN U.S.A.